THE PENNY DROPPING

Helen Farish is the author of four books of poems, *Intimates* (Cape, 2005), *Nocturnes at Nohant: The Decade of Chopin and Sand* (Bloodaxe Books, 2012), *The Dog of Memory* (Bloodaxe Books, 2016) and *The Penny Dropping* (Bloodaxe Books, 2024). *Intimates*, a Poetry Book Society Recommendation, won the Forward Prize for Best First Collection and was shortlisted for the T.S. Eliot Prize. Her PhD thesis explored the work of Louise Glück and Sharon Olds. She has taught at Sheffield Hallam University and Lancaster University, and now lives in Cumbria.

HELEN FARISH

The Penny Dropping

BLOODAXE BOOKS

Copyright © Helen Farish 2024

ISBN: 978 1 85224 996 0

First published 2024 by
Bloodaxe Books Ltd,
Eastburn,
South Park,
Hexham,
Northumberland NE46 1BS

www.bloodaxebooks.com
For further information about Bloodaxe titles
please visit our website and join our mailing list
or write to the above address for a catalogue.

Cover design: Neil Astley & Pamela Robertson-Pearce.

Printed in Great Britain by Bell & Bain Limited, Glasgow, Scotland, on
acid-free paper sourced from mills with FSC chain of custody certification.

CONTENTS

'Shall I at least set my lands in order?'

T.S. ELIOT, *The Waste Land*

'It is right to look our life accounts bravely in the face now and then, and settle them honestly.'

CHARLOTTE BRONTË, *Villette*

Things We Loved

The *Marché Central* at closing time,
men heading home on mint-laden mopeds;
walking up the marble steps to *La Poste*,
built as though communication was a god;
the Sphinx on a Saturday night,
the one-eyed rose seller, table to table
with the long stems men wanting to impress
bought by the dozen; the knife sharpener singing
outside the open classroom window;
the seamless powdery pastels of the medina;
the call to prayer; the labels in Arabic
glued to your bag before it was thrown
onto the roof of the bus; fish tagine on Fridays;
red and black taxis; the Atlantic at Ain Diab
in one of its opal moods, the football games
on the sands, the ocean thumping down its rollers,
scoring each and every time; the air in Essaouira,
glassine on the first day of spring; harira;
the cinema whose ceiling dripped as if it too felt
the weepy scenes; the slipper souk in Marrakesh,
and those acrobats twisting and looping and hooping
on the street, tumbling and rolling without fear
of what one bad move might mean. We watched
from the restaurant at whose window we sat
and where we must have known
(though we both claimed not to)
what was about to begin.

In the Balance

Full of joie de vivre, fun bubbling up – you were good at life,
like the charming friend you could have chosen over me
when it was in the balance that long weekend in Marrakech,
the three of us in the square having our fake fortunes told,
being followed round the souk by a boy who could flip
his eyeballs, sitting out the rain in the Café de Paris
with a pack of cards. But later, after dark, a man ran up
and slapped my behind so hard it stung. I yelled after him,
some old shame bubbling up. Did you observe
on that first full day we spent together how I could flip?
Confident then crumbling, full of self then empty
of self, centred then way off. But I was never fake.
I didn't set out to charm you. I never played my cards
one way or the other. I was just me falling for you.

Taste of Home

You wore it that winter's day on the Corniche.
Single-breasted, second-hand, pure new wool
in anthracite – a gentleman's overcoat.
We'd had a falling out over something I'd done.
As we walked and talked, the tide coming in, I waited
for the judgement which would cut me off.
Then you stopped, unbuttoned your coat,
opened it like the wings which were all around us
and folded me inside. We went to that shop
in Ain Diab which sold imported foods –
sometimes all you wanted was a taste of home –
buying a bar of Cadbury's fruit and nut,
a packet of McVities digestives. I opened both
in the taxi back, saw that they were long past
their 'best before', but who cared?
I'd met someone who folded me inside his coat,
who listened and forgave, for me a taste
of something new, something utterly exotic,
more foreign than any of the passing scenery.

'The Eve of St Agnes'

And if we weren't in Fez, we weren't far off,
just a bus ride, and therefore just a bus ride
from where Keats' manna and dates had grown.
Fez – succulent in his imagination
and planted in mine in a northern classroom
aged fifteen. And here I was sharing the fruits
of his poem with you in an ungreen park
amid date palms and leathery flowers in shades
of lemony cream. There were no fountains,
no ponds or pools, but still it was an oasis
in the city we'd shortened to 'Casa'.
And if I'm thinking of the park and reading Keats
aloud to one another like dreamy lovers,
we must have been dreamy lovers and therefore
it was May or June, July, the honeyed time
when I was living more at yours than mine.
I'd found it somehow in that brick-dusty city
with its shops where the owners stood outside –
the school-uniform-navy hard-backed Keats
which was plain but for his name written
in silver on the spine. And when the joys
of all my life are said and sung, and when
I have mickle time to grieve, and when
my passing-bell may ere the midnight toll,
and when what we were to each other has fled,
ay, ages long ago, let it come once more,
sudden, like the full-blown roses the park
had none of, that morning when we discovered
that the delicates of the language were
one more thing that we could pass between us.

Exposure

We're visiting the medieval tannery in Fez.
In your left hand is a red camera being held
as though you'd be surprised to find it there.
Your white shirt is long-sleeved and tailored
despite the heat, despite it being a place
of searing exposure, devoid of shelter.
You seem as unaware of me taking your photo
as you are of the camera in your own hand,
as though you're too lost to even think
of finding yourself again by taking
the pictures you always take.
We'd been given carte blanche to wander round –
nowhere out of bounds – with only one young guide
who seemed as out of his depth as we were,
as though tourists were as rare and troubling
as clouds. In the photo, it's your utter lostness,
your dereliction of yourself which I love.
Just a fluke I caught you tilting on the rim
of one of the stone vats that there should surely
have been barriers around. Just a fluke I caught you
when you'd taken all your own barriers down,
a risk of such enormity, falling into a vat
of dun-coloured dye paled by comparison.

The Innocence of Pronouns

No washing but ours in the courtyard, the street door
only ever slamming cheerfully behind you or me,
never any light cracking through the shutters
of the apartment below ours. Yet there she was,
springing on us as we returned laden from the market,
the neighbour we didn't know we had.
'*Voi due mi avete disturbato*,' she said –
Voi, you two, have been disturbing me, *mi* singular.
We were in Italy together for the first time,
what would we listen to but opera? Verdi, Puccini,
Bellini, Donizetti, choruses, duets, arias, which had fallen
through the ancient floorboards and into the rooms
of the ancient (as she appeared to us) woman below.
There was so little of her to disturb, such a spare frame,
shoulder-length grey hair, a face scored with suffering.
And we, *noi*, us two, had caused her more suffering.
Were we students, she asked, at the Conservatorio?
It's only now that I think of her living alone
in a lightless apartment while you and I
came and went, always together,
turning the volume down but still filling
our weekend mornings with tapes of bel canto.
Even now if the radio springs 'Casta Diva' on me
(me singular), the opening arpeggios are so laden
I drop everything just to listen once more.

Mozart's 233rd Birthday

It was standing room only at the back of the church,
but we were warmed by all the furs Sicilian women
hunted out for such occasions – classical music, christenings.
Christopher Warren-Green and the London Chamber Orchestra
performing Eine Kleine Nachtmusik as though discovering it,
as though Mozart had rushed in with the score that morning,
out of breath after running the length of Via Maqueda,
past the Quattro Canti destined to be scaffolded
for the entire year the city was our home,
past your barber's, past the best place for *gelato*,
past the fountain on whose steps we'd sit on Sundays,
past that church whose dome turned the unreliable
turquoise of old copper when it rained, past Gigi's,
past Piazza Bellini and that giant ad for São coffee –
Con tutto il sapore dei giorni più belli –
past the public phone plastered with photos of the man shot
as he searched his pockets for *gettoni*.
We all know how memory orchestrates the past,
but I don't believe Mozart could have had a better birthday
before or since. The applause! The cries of *Bravo! Encore!*
And for our own encore – a late dinner at home,
a bottle of *Donnafugata* we finished off in bed.
On my own 233rd birthday, I'll remember it all as keenly
as if the final chord still vibrated on the strings,
as if the holy water in its stone bowl by the entrance
was still depleted by fingers dipping in before praying
for blessings. If my own fingers weren't among them,
believe me, it was only because I wouldn't have known
what else to ask for.

Premonition

It wasn't my parents' plane which fell from the sky,
but Pan Am flight 103 exploding fifteen miles
from their home, by which time
my parents were themselves airborne,
my father having boarded the plane believing
they wouldn't arrive, but unable to let me down,
unable to say he'd had a premonition, they couldn't come.
After all, he knew the lengths we'd gone to –
moving rooms, spending 60,000 lire on a tree,
stuffing the kitchen with panettone, ricotta, ravioli,
bowls of clementines and sweet Marsala wine.
You'd bought poinsettias for the courtyard,
hung lights which spelled out *BUON NATALE*.
PS my father had written in the letter addressed to me
the night before they left home and which he would have placed
on the kitchen table, the seersucker cloth my mother was sure
to have shaken one last time before closing the door behind them;
PS he'd written after telling me that all they had was mine
and I mustn't grieve for long but must pick up the pieces
and enjoy life again; *PS* he'd written, it was his wish,
close to his heart, that I'd marry you because I couldn't hope
to meet anyone kinder, more loyal, more loving.
It would be a weight off his mind, is what he was saying,
a weight off his mind as he fell from the sky.
But he never got to give me away,
and now the chances are I'll be his to the end.

The Sirocco

I'd only ever encountered the wind
(until that evening) in literature,
in novels and in the accounts
of travellers to southern lands,
but from *Death in Venice* on, I'd loved
its name, and from that evening on
I no longer had to imagine
how it would be living in a city
the wind visited, a city whose residents
lamented with limp hands its arrival,
attaching to it the same words
they had always all their lives attached,
but which never lost potency or slackened,
remaining as fresh as the wind was not,
with its sticky heat and desert colours –
a brown pink, a peach the colour of a peach
which fell from the tree days before –
and I remember us lingering on our street
after the evening was over, feeling a thrill,
feeling like characters in a novella,
until our neighbour came out in a dressing gown
to put the day's rubbish on her step and cursed
the curses she must always curse
when the wind snatched it from her hands
and bounced it down the hill,
the tightly-tied plastic bag from *Standa*.

Qui e Li

Much of what we discarded still had life in it,
and on that last morning the bags we'd placed
in the street the night before had been opened.
In our quarter of the old quarter, there were those
on the breadline, like the men pushing barrows
of pirated cassettes round the streets
so that 'Eye of the Tiger', 'Born to Run',
or 'Ain't Nobody' would often blast in
through balcony doors making me put down
my pen. And I may as well have left it there
because almost all those poems written
throughout the year ended up on the doorstep
on our final night; when push came to shove
they didn't seem worth packing.
And whoever sorted through our bin bags
didn't want the poems either, scattering
the sheets of A4 so that the last thing I saw
as our taxi revved up the narrow street –
a *salita*, not a *via*, with paving stones
the colour of parchment, washing on balconies
already drying, the *zucchero* seller warming up
his voice, the stray dog sniffing his way
to the market where we'd said goodbye
to the baker the day before – the last thing
I saw under the blank blue of another day
as the *Gesù* chimed eight, was my orphaned poems,
fending for themselves, being blown *qui e li*.
Of course I wanted them back then,
like I wanted our keys back, our decision to leave
back, like I wanted the day before yesterday
and the one before that back, and each
and every one of those mornings in my study
so I could put my pen down and go find you,
rewriting all my wrongs.

The Halcyon Days

The snow did away with itself overnight,
telling the north no point letting its weather
slip south again until the warmth
decreed by Zeus was over:
eight days of summer in winter,
December's debris swiftly swept aside,
tables placed outdoors for lunch,
tables on which things got left behind –
dark glasses, fish heads, the hollowed halves
of lemons, a drop of house white
in the carafe – the city's lunch hour
always plural, always two paired
companionably side by side.
We were living somewhere
where the weather obeyed the myth,
where the gods, visible on their mountain-top
across the bay, were in beneficent mood.
I've spent years asking what happened
to those companionable hours, the ones
which felt they were gifted by Zeus
and which themselves have acquired
the quality of myth. There are thoughts
it behoves mortals to swiftly sweep aside,
such as, *What if? What if?*
and *What's the use? What's the use?*

Snow on the Road to Naoussa

It's the winter drives that come back to me,
us listening to Rembetiko or *Astral Weeks*,
the air shorn of haze, horses standing still
in pale fields, the roads quiet enough
for attendants at filling stations to read
chapters of *The Odyssey* between customers
to whom they'd serve Nescafé with Noy-Noy.
We'd drink it on empty forecourts, reading signs,
place names, distances, locating ourselves.
Your ex sent a card from Mandalay with two words:
Fancy that! Pulling up in some Balkan backwater –
Serres, Komotini, Kozani – *Fancy that!* we'd say.
She was a foreign correspondent. What was I?
A passenger, slipped under the radar, undetected
by the kind of life that acquires a capital L.
The inert winter violet of those hills in Thessaly
as though in all their history there'd never been
a decisive moment, snow on the road to Naoussa,
miles of undulating tan-coloured fields near Farsala
which caused our car to mysteriously slow
as though the farmer had ploughed up melancholy,
homesickness. And the drive to Athos that January,
its soundless soundtrack, a fudgy sun flicking
between trees – *now you see me, now you don't* –
and the monk who raised a distant hand
from beyond the point of no return.

Christ Has Risen! He Has Risen Indeed!

You ate tripe soup. It was traditional
on Orthodox Easter Eve. A table with space
for a dozen or more, all the generations,
then us two strangers turning up late
in need of a room, swiftly invited
to the gathering. How happy you were
at that table, how at ease as everyone
squeezed up, how good with the little ones.
We followed to the church, the village in darkness,
the church too until the priest gave the sign
and one lit candle was source enough
to light two hundred more.
Christos Anesti! Alithos Anesti!
If you had proposed that night
I'd have said *Yes, yes indeed*,
because the self who felt she could
take part and partake had risen.
But maybe all you saw were the signs –
I'd said no to the tripe and only joined in
for one glass of *tsikoudia*
before going back to our room to write.
Things rise and fall – moments, places, selves.
We waved goodbye next morning, driving off
into the empty interior, high-soaring
solitary birds, little or no sign anywhere
of human hand.

Day of Miracles

A long trek across a remote valley,
said *The Blue Guide to Crete*,
but the frescoes would be ample reward.
And the day we chose was itself worshipful,
glorious, a farmer's wife feeding us
black olives, salty white cheese,
honey from her own hives.
Years later you began drawing then painting.
Alleluia, I thought, alleluia to making art
as well as pursuing it along stony tracks
through citrus groves and scrubland
and juniper-covered slopes and meadows
which would have had Monet himself
setting up his easel, not one thing to complain of,
no wind, no cloud, the temperature poppy-perfect.
The church had been left open to the elements,
the frescoes crumbling, but the fish in their basket
looked as though they'd just been caught,
as though, at any moment, they might leap
into the blue sky swimming in through the hole
in the ceiling of tumbling stars. Day of miracles –
walking through a Monet, being treated like royalty
by a stranger, looking fifteenth-century fish in the eye,
fish not in the mood to multiply for anyone,
even such a slender boy-like Christ. 'Shall we go?'
I said to my slender and still boy-like lover,
the flowers springing back up in his wake.

Filling Station, Crete

I'd have liked a wedding among strangers,
no one to cry, no one saying 'I remember the time',
no one to worry about, no one to half
breakdown as my father did at his other
daughter's wedding, no one appraising
my figure in the dress or saying my hairdo
was a mistake, no wedding albums, lists,
thank you notes, no sense of a rite of passage
because there'd be no one there who knew
anything of my journey, and if the living
weren't invited, the dead
wouldn't be there either.
And I'd have liked the venue to be
some unprepossessing place
like that wedding you and I stumbled upon
in a large function room attached
to a filling station in the middle of nowhere.
Why weren't we turned away?
Why were we welcomed as though invited,
as though the event wouldn't have been complete
without our witness? Chagall lifted the bride
and groom a foot off the concrete floor
when they danced the first dance.
It was so hot on that trip I often wore white
and that day nothing would have been more right
than to have made our vows
in a filling station function room
full of strangers, the priest
only two tables away.
I wouldn't have hesitated and I wouldn't
have woken the next morning asking
what on earth had possessed me.

P

Bella Vista! Panorama! Vue Panoramique!
Any other country would have signposted
the kind of places we found by chance
or instinct, and were always hopeful
(despite the lack of signs) of finding again.
We'd measure kilometres to the nearest town,
write it on the map, circle it, make notes,
as though we didn't doubt we'd be driving
along that evergreen road, through those hills,
or walking to that stumbled-upon viewpoint
again one day. So when I open those old maps,
in the vastness I sometimes stumble upon
a 4.7km in your neat hand, a 'P' circled, an arrow.
But even as your pen hovered over the map,
'P' stood not for where to park, but for the Past,
and the arrow only poignant, not practical.
This way back to something unrepeatable!
This way back to that moment we stood united,
the evening so still we heard the hills breathing;
that moment of looking towards the glitter,
the spangled end of land we hadn't known
would be ending! Oh! The exclamation marks
pouring out of our mouths!

May Day

You would have joined in, whereas I wanted to take it in
from the terrace of our holiday let which offered a perfect view
of the village tables stuck together for May Day,
a green wreath crowning the man with the lyre.
Poor you, stuck with me, who preferred it all
at one remove, a periphery creature like the Scops owl.
The gathering was intimate yet public, spontaneous
and yet depended upon; something – the world, life, love –
would have been out of joint had the lyre not been magicked
from under a chair, had honey-coloured wine not softened
a night already almost too tender to touch.
I should have said *You go*. It seems obvious, a simple solution.
And I'd have watched as they crowned you with the wreath
of tamarisk and bay and carob and gleaming citrus, glint
of olive-silver, all the wild flowers of the field woven in.
But you were too much the gentleman to leave my side.
And so you stayed, observing merriment from a distance,
trying to catch the echoes of song, until finally, years later,
cries of *Mayday! Mayday!* could be heard echoing through our house.

From the Album

We are wearing blue and white and the house
behind us is blue and white and the cloths
on most café tables are blue and white check.
And the flag often in the background waving
from terraces or squares or planted in the sand
is blue and white. Likewise the sea and sky.
And a blue flower (a stranger we can't name)
lines the path to our door, the path the white cat
slinks along each morning, chancing it, hoping
for a saucer of milk. Inside, the floor is tiled blue
against the white of the bed. We took photos
of everything on this trip. But after someone else
came along, chancing it, and after you planted
your flag elsewhere, you declined to take with you
a single colour snap, nothing to challenge
the black and white, the likewise of your memories.
But I remember how the privacy afforded
by the blue diamonds on the white lace curtains
of our ground floor room was useful
those afternoons we returned from the beach
to crumple the sheets. In fact, now I look harder,
our skin in the photo has that flush, that afterglow,
my blue eyes dreamy, unfocused,
as though I'd just been licking my lips.

Burning

You are someone who once slept
under an olive tree, and I lay awake
in the shade we'd partitioned,
glad to be awake because that meant
I wasn't missing the time you slept
under an olive tree. Fancy that, I thought,
a life in which you sleep deep
in Arkadian country, a quiet grove,
not a care in the rest of the world,
at peace under your Panama.
Let the bees buzz, let the cicadas cicada,
the crickets cricket, for I alone
am the keeper of that hour and I alone
know that as the shade moved across you
I saved you from burning by taking off my shirt
to lay it over your bare arm.
Of the woman you fell for after me,
There isn't the same fire, you said,
as though, despite all my ministrations,
all my care, I'd somehow burnt you.

Legacy

I called her 'wormy lips' as though I knew
that when I left you alone for another month
she'd try to worm her way in. 'Where is she then?'
she'd said when you'd reminded her of my existence.
But she was right. I should have been by your side,
and this is what you hoped I'd glean from the story,
which of course – being me – I missed entirely. Instead,
I acquired a dislike of women called Claire with an 'i'.
And before her, in the bookshop, a colleague of yours
who admired my 'cool' socks. Clearly, when asking herself
what you saw in me and why you'd turned her down,
this is what she'd come up with: it must be her socks.
And after her, the violin teacher fluttering her eyelashes
in a Scottish accent you found charming.
The legacy of that one is a mistrust of anyone
who calls a violin a fiddle. And after you'd moved out,
a friend told me you'd once placed your hands
on her shoulders, turning her to face you.
'He didn't kiss me, though', she'd said.
But I never saw any of these women as a threat,
and I was right. When you turned our friend
to look her in the eyes, she was only a substitute me.
Because, as Claire with an 'i' said, *Where was I?*
Even when physically present, I was absent.
Like my mother. Except surely not – not me –
passing on a legacy of loneliness.

The Right Thing

Your ghost keeps me awake now as you kept me awake
those nights when you were sick, when your breath came
too quickly, your temperature climbed and your muscles
wrapped you in pain. But still you refused a doctor.
Maybe tomorrow, you said. No, I said. Today, now.
And I remember the doctor who came, his wild grey hair
and his deadly serious face as he called for the ambulance
which carried you off from our rented bed
in our rented upper floor of an old house in Old Headington.
Your instinct was right, the doctor said as the ambulance
squeezed down the lane best suited to bikes.
Meningitis can be a killer, he said, you may have saved
your husband's life. I didn't contradict 'my husband',
I let it stand, seeing myself on the church steps,
adjusting my long white train. One more day, I thought,
of going without treatment, and all that you were
could have been lost, and it would have happened
on my watch. What would I have said to your mother?
So when I think, as I have of late, that I never apologised
to your parents for getting so much wrong,
I remember the words that came out of the mouth
of the doctor with the wild spirals of iron-grey hair,
the doctor who had married us. All my life
I've hugged to myself the times when I've been told
I've done the right thing. You did the right thing,
the doctor said, you did the right thing.

Valentine's Day

It was Valentine's Day in the era before
people carried phones. I didn't know
what to do other than stand watching
at the bay window. Our street was a cul-de-sac,
the gate at the end opening into a park
which led into woodland, paths we explored
every weekend. In autumn I loved to hear
the shouts of schoolboy football
starting up again, and in mid-February
the songs of birds singing as though
not quite trusting their own urge.
Standing at the window, looking at parked cars,
the bare buddleia in our square of garden,
the flopped crocuses, the inherited quince
I'd pruned too hard, I thought of our neighbour
leaving her back door open day and night.
What if he comes back and I don't hear?
she'd said to me. *I couldn't live with myself.*
I waited and waited, forgot the dinner,
the wine already breathing, your gift,
the card in its red envelope, the candles
burning down. Then I saw you. Thanks to a puncture,
you'd pushed your bike all the way home.
So you weren't in A&E, your bike mangled
on Magdalen Bridge, the contents of your backpack
scattered in the rain, being driven over
in the headlit dusk. And how could I have imagined
even for a moment that there was someone else,
the pair of you having a clandestine drink,
sequestered in a snug at The Eagle and Child?
How could I have thought such a thing,
braced at the bay window as though
at the prow of a ship, the sea outside
immense, dark, encroaching, and me
tossed about on the waves of my imagining?

Flowers, Baguettes, *Fromage*, Wine

There's some very Parisian rain
on the Thursday, otherwise it's the sun
which styles the city. Winter here means
white jeans, ankle boots with heels,
scarves with attitude. Cecile has given us
her attic for the week, with its tribal masks,
wall hangings, chic plants, maps with pins
for where she has been and where
life will take her next. There's a sloping ceiling
in the bedroom for whoever is on top
to comically hit their head.
Rue de la Boule Rouge, fifth floor, carrying up
flowers, baguettes, *fromage*, wine.
We are working out who we are now,
as though this is something to be done
every seven years, during which time
our bodies have replaced each and every cell,
so that the ones which bruise when we hit
our heads are not the same ones
which bruised when we first met.
Style it any which way you want,
we are happy, something you put down
to me being myself again. But then you play
(on the wet day) the Well-Tempered Clavier,
the first prelude, those broken chords
in the rain, and I've never been so sad
to be happy.

'Pretty Woman'

It was as near as dammit the dress
Julia Roberts wore to the polo match,
except mine was navy with cream
polka dots, hers caramel and cream.
I'd been shopping with your brother's wife
in *Jigsaw*, so you'd not seen the dress
till I stood, slinky, against the back door.
You left whatever it was you were doing
in the garden – it was August, so let's say
you were dead-heading – and very quickly
I was no longer wearing the dress.
And if I had known that that was the last time,
surely I would have woken up to the enormity
of what I was letting slip, and fought hard,
fought with every fibre, to stop it.
We were made for each other like polkas and dots,
caramel and cream, Julia Roberts and Richard Gere.
But look at me stepping back into the dress,
pulling up the side zip, smoothing it down,
as though that's all it took.

A Hundred Days

We had a hundred days left,
but the photos of our last holiday
are full of fun, mischief even, like that visit
to Ancy-le-Franc, the château where all the staff
had gone home bar the woman on the door.
It was off-season, late afternoon, the place empty.
There was no one to tell us not to touch,
so we touched, posing like kings and queens
haughty on roomy velvet chairs, chasing
along statued corridors, helping ourselves
to the banquet which only looked fake close-up,
lifting goblets to our mouths as though drunk
on the emptiness inside. In the formal gardens
I posed patiently while you walked so far away
I became not much more than a speck.
I've always loved the title of that film about Anne Boleyn,
Anne of a Thousand Days. I look back at the photos
of all the châteaux we toured that September,
all the palaces and fountains, the picturesque
breakfasts, the winding streets, the vineyards,
the photos of us, heads together,
looking like the real thing, and all the while
I had a hundred days left. A hundred days,
and then the axe fell.

That Route

I remember that time we were driving back home
after visiting friends who had young children and I said
how glad I was we hadn't gone down that route,
adding a rhetorical 'Aren't you?' I was at the wheel.
Did I make some manoeuvre, switch lanes perhaps,
as a way to breeze past the reply I hadn't expected?
We were on the M40 on a late November
late afternoon, waning light, rain turning to sleet,
and the weather had been no doubt partly to blame
for why keeping small children happy in a cheerless
south London park had seemed like a fate anyone
would be relieved to have escaped. Tears on the seesaw,
fights on the swings, injuries on the slide, more tears.
But you had smiled through it all, volunteering
piggybacks and peek-a-boo and pushes on the swings.
High Wycombe, Aylesbury, Thornhill Park and Ride.
There were never any tears or fights in our house
until the night, two weeks later, you wept like a child.

The Butcher's Boy

The story behind the story of the butcher's boy
is that it wasn't the butcher's boy you were crying for.
His story was a hook, like one of those in-your-face hooks
for hanging meat, which I nevertheless succeeded
in not seeing until yesterday when suffering
my own onslaught of grief, at the end of which
came the memory of you weeping over the story
of the sixteen-year-old butcher's boy,
his father's love for him, the affability of the boy,
his winning smiles despite hating handling meat,
a tender-hearted boy who said sorry when slicing off ears,
cutting out tongues, and the father's regret
at pushing the son into the family trade,
not listening, and how the boy then took the first
opportunity out, signing up, a soldier, dead
in the first week of the Somme, cut up
by the barbed wire, then taken apart by a shell –
the memory of you so moved by this story,
the way one tragedy is picked from an otherwise
incomprehensible number and flesh put on it
to help us imagine something off the scale.
But imagine how hard it would have been
for the father to willingly let his only son enter
another trade when he was offering him
a ready-made living, one he'd broken his back
to build up, thinking he'd done everything right,
done things by the book. He'd only just added the boy
to the name of the shop: *Turnbull & Son*.
I remember when you finally had the courage
to tell me your plan of action, one of the hardest things,
you said, was how long my name had been linked
with yours, in the same breath, as though we came
ready-made.

The Candle Snuffer

Habitat persuaded me we needed
a candle snuffer. It was in my bag
when I knocked on our front door, hands full.
Table linen, pointless baskets, a spaghetti server –
what had happened to the undomesticated me
you'd fallen for, the me with her bare
fourth floor apartment, the kitchen I never once
cooked in, where wine and water were drunk
from the same glass, where I'd yet to care
about the thread-count of sheets, the benefits
of double-lined blinds? We'd had seven addresses
and now we were home-making; if we bought clutter
there was somewhere to put it.
Oh blessed and happy hour in *Habitat* on Botley Road
when all our rooms were ideal in my head,
where they glowed safe from harm,
where I couldn't have conceived of myself
on the futon in the spare room that very night.
For years, I never thought about our house
or how lucky we were that our taste coincided
so that I could shop alone confident
that you would see the necessity
or be equally gratified by the beauty.
A wrought-iron candle snuffer:
Give it here, you said, let me see if it works.

The Penny Dropping

When the penny drops, you don't drop
a penny, you drop whatever it is
you happen to be holding.
So when the penny dropped
that my mother was dying,
that she was in hospital not to be healed,
but simply to be turned and cleaned
and medicated till she died –
standing there at the nurses' station, I dropped
the yoghurt pots. I needed all of me:
I needed my hands and my forearms and my shoulders,
I needed my fingernails and my eyelashes,
I needed my cartilage and all my sinews and muscles
in order to bear the understanding, I could not also
bear the weight of the yoghurt
(which in any case my mother had spurned).
And so it was with you, though you happened
to be holding a glass when you understood
that you couldn't continue, that the moment had come
and it was anguish. I'd looked so happy, you said,
knocking on our front door, both hands
clutching shopping, keys deep in my bag;
I'd looked so happy to see you
when you'd let me in that evening.
For years I didn't understand how the glass
could have left your hands without your say-so.
I believed there must have been anger, the intent to shock,
or if not, then perhaps while breaking us
you also needed to break something material,
a nothing-thing, just a glass
from which we had both drunk
and which could now be spurned.

In Seville That Spring

In Seville that spring you'd fallen
face forward into your food, blacking out
slapstick-style. I remember waiters flapping,
a doctor coming, but we never did get to the truth
of why, what happened in your brain
that you were mildly unwell one moment,
the next unconscious. And it was like that with us –
one minute we were home-making, the next
you were on the floor, couldn't go on,
you wanted space. I gave you space,
but I should have stayed, sticking to you
like the paella I'd picked from your hair.
I should have made you talk to me,
should have fought for you, stomping my feet,
raising my arms high above my head,
joining my fingertips, teardrop-style.
I should have flounced, shaken and lifted
my skirts like the woman in Seville
singing *Por favor, mi amor, por favor*.
Instead, British-style, I drove north,
three hundred miles, not even conscious
of the mistake I was making, the life
which wouldn't be there when I returned.

Scapegoat

I remember the time my mother phoned
to accuse me of hoovering up her earrings,
her treasured clip-ons from the 1950s.
You must have been careless, she said,
the last time you were hoovering, I didn't ask you
to get the hoover out, I'm tired of people
hoovering for me without my say-so, and now
you've hoovered up the earrings which I know
were on my dressing table.
My mother in her seventies was as upset as I'd been
aged seven or eight, when I split open the beaded purse
I'd got for Christmas. I had worn it out with love,
zipping it, unzipping it, zipping it, unzipping it.
My mother had always done all her raging
and grieving on the spot, clipping it onto
whoever was near. *My treasured earrings,*
must even they be taken from me?
Now she had a box, a plush-lined claret-coloured box
with a silver hinge, but nothing inside.
I aways had guilt inside, so I knew when I lost him
that it was my fault, that I had worn out
his love for me. Worn it out, that treasured
beaded bejewelled gilded thing
I never believed I deserved.

That Postcard You Sent from Crete

Maybe it was the light, the way in Crete
it seems haunted by itself. Or maybe you stroked
the comforting felt ears of a donkey,
its olive-black eyes looking into yours, saying,
Don't forget how she always did her best.
Maybe, as you ate outdoors, it was the cats
edging closer, hoping for a fish head or tail,
and you remembered how I always fed them,
tossing scraps under taverna tables.
Maybe *Mavrodafne* was on the wine list.
Maybe you returned to the Mesará plain,
then that place on the south coast, and the sea said,
Do you remember how she loved me,
how happy I made her? Or maybe it was the ache
of the island's interior, the mountain roads
making white the loneliest colour until dusk
when the light recast itself into a violet-mauve
which could only be seen when your gaze
slid off to the side. Maybe the jasmine was out
or the frangipani. Maybe the sun was falling
through the slatted cover of a café terrace
and the stripes of afternoon amber on the table
pulled at your heart, helpless as they were
to stop themselves undoing their own design.
From the rack of dusty postcards you chose one
which was all background, fold after fold
of unpopulated hills. Anyway, for whatever reason,
Crete prompted some warmth towards me
back in Blighty, even if, now I think of it, your words
could have been read as scraps under the table.
'I've been thinking about the early years,'
you wrote, 'the good times.' What did it matter?
Heads or tails, I'd already lost the toss.

On Approval

That day we spent in Bath, it was your suggestion
a few weeks after you'd moved out. I didn't enjoy
a minute of it. There wasn't a minute of it where
I didn't feel like one of the items my mother
brought home 'on approval' from *Bulloughs*,
things which might live with us for two weeks –
a lamp, a bedside table, a dress coat, a rug,
shoes I'd set my heart on – then be disapproved of
and returned. And for those two weeks
the items knew their fate was in the balance.
Look how brightly I'm shining, said the lamp,
how I illuminate this corner to perfection!
How will you live without me, asked the bedside table,
now that I have accommodated your books,
your medications? The slub-silk dress coat said,
Admit it, I make you feel like a million dollars!
And the rug said, *Come on, walk all over me.*
That day in Bath I tried to be perfect: Don't I shine?
Don't we accommodate each other to perfection?
How will you live without me? But driving us back –
you to your new address, me to our old one –
in the brittle splintery light of March when the clocks
have changed, all I felt was walked over.
Thank goodness for my new shoes, the ones
I wouldn't be returning. Black patent leather
with a Jacobean buckle and the kind of heel
that means business.

My Exit

The night I heard you were engaged
I drove home, missing my exit
at a roundabout I knew
like the back of my ringless hand.
Cowley, London, Barton, Marston,
Headington, Risinghurst, Cowley.
As I went round again, Pachelbel's Canon
came on the radio and it was very late
and I was wiping my eyes and someone
zoomed up behind me at a crazy speed
and I missed my exit again.
It was going round and round in my head,
how I'd taken it for granted
when you'd said you'd like us
to be married, how I'd assumed
there was no rush. London, Cowley,
Marston, Barton. And now someone else
had zoomed up behind us at a crazy speed.
Risinghurst, Headington, City Centre.
The Big Day, Wedlock, Married Life.
Did it matter which exit I took
now I'd missed the one meant for me?

Thanking the Universe

If I'd heard of some woman
breaking your heart, treating
you badly, being careless, too dumb
to see their luck in being given
a chance with you; if I'd heard
of some woman taking you for granted,
not cherishing you, not paying
enough attention, not drawing
you out, reading the signs –
even in my cast-off state
I'd have been outraged,
I'd have wanted to find her, to say
How dare you cause him pain?
But luckily, the very next woman you met
thanked the universe and all the stars
and the planets and galaxies and deep time,
and she thanked your parents,
she thanked the corporate restructuring
which was responsible for your relocation
to the publisher's where she worked,
she thanked her singledom, she thanked
the designers of the dress you noticed
as she crossed the office,
she thanked Jesus for being born
at Christmas and the subsequent tradition
of office Christmas parties, she thanked
her earthly father for imprinting on her psyche
the blueprint of Tall, Dark, Handsome.
But I like to believe she loved you too much
to thank me, author
of your unhappiness. And so, tell me,
do I have to thank the universe that you met
someone who reversed the narrative,
who made you so happy you wanted

to marry her and stay married
for the rest of your life, for all time,
deep and shallow? I do.

Fairytale

When you left I thought I'd meet another you,
but I met the opposite, and the opposite,
and another opposite, until I forgot
what the opposite of the opposite was like:
someone who phoned when they said they would phone,
who loved to spend the day not just the night,
who would write *I love you* two hundred times
on as many squares of loo roll leading to the bedroom.
No one had ever been more in need than me
of waking up to their luck, what they'd been given,
of playing their part, snapping out of
whatever dark trance they had fallen into.
I look at your lovely princess online.
Too late now for me to rise and shine.

The Waste Land

Eliot, the popular and sizeable polar bear
who'd refused to fit into the overhead lockers,
was sitting on my knee drawing oohs and aahs
from the hostesses as though I'd given birth.
I'd christened him following a staffroom argument
at the school we'd just left: poetry so elitist
and complicated – why teach it now?
Soft toys and teddy bears, I'd never seen the point,
yet Eliot accompanied you and me from address
to address, until, when I was living alone,
a friend's child couldn't stop sobbing
when the time came to part from him.
'Take him,' I said, 'he wants to be with you now.'
How I missed that polar bear!
But for a long time after you left I was like that,
performing regular small acts of self-harm.
Cast off, sent out into the cold
without so much as a word of thanks
for all the fun, all the years –
not even a wave from the doorstep.
Why push me away when you love me?
It's complicated, I said.

Original You

You changed your name after you left
as though to be doubly sure you wouldn't hear
anyone calling for the original you,
as though removing yourself physically
wasn't enough, you wanted another layer
of removal, a belt and braces approach
so that if the past came calling
you wouldn't turn round or if you did
it would only be to say *Who?*
In the city where we met, I've a photo
of original you wearing forest-green braces
over a purple and white striped shirt.
It was a city where names tripped you up,
deceived you, where the only street maps on sale
belonged to the old king's reign, printing
yet to catch up with his son's rechristening
of chosen streets, stations, boulevards.
So when I was running and lost, unable to find
the bus station where you were waiting,
I drew blanks from locals. *Where?* they said,
sensitive to the forced loss of the original name.
Where? they said, hostile to its usurper.
It was prayer that got me to the long-distance bus
just as the wheels were turning.
The city had tried to wrongfoot me, to trick me,
but irrespective of the official and the colloquial,
of new and old, of Arabic and French,
of painted-over signs and numerical sequences
out of sequence, nothing was going to stop me
walking down the aisle to the back row
where you sat, enthroned, beaming
as I took my place, everything
in its sequence, no gap between love
and what I saw printed on your face.

No Point Now

It's not as if it's years ago
and I'm living on rue de Cabris
and you're living on rue de la Somme
and if we'd had a misunderstanding
and I'd gone home alone and then thought
of what I should have said,
I'd walk in the dark, against all advice,
the half hour between rue de Cabris
and rue de la Somme because the other advice
was never get into a taxi alone.
Women vanished from the streets
when shops and businesses closed
and there was nothing on offer
but enjoyment. And yet the risk
of waiting till morning to say
what I needed to say
felt like the greater risk –
leaving you hurt, allowing you to dwell –
and there were no phones in our pockets
or our homes. I remember once,
at the intersection called Mers Sultan,
a motorcyclist grabbing me, me thinking
this is it, before a taxi driver
put his hand on his horn
and left it there. The motorcyclist
let go and the taxi driver gave me
a free ride and lots of free advice,
first in one language, then the other,
French to Arabic and back, making
his point then making it again.
Each night now I lie
in safety, wouldn't dream
of putting myself in harm's way.
Yet at the intersection of night
and day, along come these poems,

blowing their horns, waking me
with their own urgent advice,
half a lifetime too late –
You need to say this to him and this! –
as though no one has told them,
and I haven't the heart to say,
No point now.

Triggers

Every time I eat *Pasta alla Gorgonzola*;
every wedding I've been to; when a once
mutual friend died; my sixtieth birthday;
January the 2nd; returning to the Peloponnese;
all the times I've not returned to Sicily;
whenever I fall for someone else.
But why yesterday, a bog standard Tuesday?
It must have been the stag, the young stag
who appeared in my garden, eating the leaves
of the apple tree before falling asleep
in its shade. He slept so soundly and so long
I began to take his presence for granted
and I drifted off. When I returned
he'd vanished, as though my absorbed gaze
was all that had held him there.
I felt cheated then. Was that the trigger?
I never would believe that you cheated.
It seemed as remote a possibility as a stag sleeping
outside my kitchen window, sated on sweet leaves
and warmed by an apple-red sun.
But then only last month someone told me something
about you, which (caught in my own trap!),
I have to believe, otherwise there was no sleeping stag
and no rhyme or reason to the triggering of grief.

Pasta alla Gorgonzola

If I can't find Gorgonzola picante
I use Stilton or Blacksticks Blue.
The wine – a bold Italian red.
The penne should be slow-dried,
bronze drawn. Butter, cream – easy.
Take three ingredients – pasta, wine, you.
Add a fourth – Christmas Eve, a birthday,
a promotion. Valentine's day. An anniversary.
Toss me a day in 1989, early spring, Cefalú,
lunch which friends threw together
in ten minutes flat, a recipe we never forgot.
For dessert, oranges from their garden.
This is how to live, we thought.
We *both* thought, This is how to live.

The Shaman Says

The Shaman says she sees us, you and me,
in the Elysian fields, somewhere
the Shaman rarely gets taken.
And we are so happy, you and I,
the Shaman says, just talking,
the pair of us, as though
we've known each other forever –
since the Middle Ages,
the Shaman says, that's how long.
The Shaman looks happy too.
Oh, it's lovely, she says, such a treat
to see two souls so at one.
I am rising in the Shaman's estimation
because I didn't just bring
a broken heart, I brought a broken heart
which is whole elsewhere.
The Shaman says it's immaterial
whether or not I see you again in this life.
Not long ago (last century)
these words would have made my whole heart
break once more – never to see you again
in this life, this flesh and blood life?
But fast forward to today,
and I'll take togetherness with you
wherever, whenever, on any plane.
I almost feel sorry for your wife
who only has you for the remainder
of this lifetime, this poky little corner
of the twenty-first century.

How Brilliant Is That?

You'd find me much as you left me –
walking, reading, playing the piano.
I spent months learning Bach's
B minor Fugue; when I play it snow falls
onto a cobbled street and I hear Bach
blocking out the intrusion of a servant
come to tend the fire.
Since our cat died, I lost another.
I lost my mother, my brother and three friends,
one of whom you met in the same moment
you met me. Do you remember
her long blonde hair, her panache,
her American let's-do-it style?
Two months after her 50th birthday,
an inoperable tumour. You'd recognise
six of the pictures on my walls
from when they hung on our walls;
the other sixty-seven not.
I permit you a wry smile about the fact
that I finally have no neighbours,
but no extra pairs of hands either
to carry logs, tend the fire, shovel snow,
diagnose the needs of the lawn mower.
I turn my attention from fugue
to fallen tree, from sonnet sequence
to shades of mortar grout.
Dear person who was always on my side
when you were by my side, I've learnt this:
that I had undiagnosed PTSD, four letters
that might have saved us.
So it's not, after all, true that you'd find me
as you left me. The woman you left has gone,
though I don't blame her in any way.
Her illness was operable – how brilliant is that?

Anniversary

If it was a notable anniversary –
ten years ago, I could say, or twenty –
something with a ring. Or the date itself.
But as it is none of these, tell me why
this grief now? Give me something
to pin it on, like I bumped into so-and-so
who filled me in on your new life,
or I revisited an old address, wandered
the same streets, or your photo
fell out of a book or a diary.
None of these. Not even a dream.
Just a day when I relived how you'd walked
down the stairs carrying a case packed
with things you couldn't live without,
and how impatient you were
with my surprise, with my dumb
dumbfoundedness.
It's your heart, I was told at A&E
a year ago, and how had I not noticed
the symptoms?
How had you not noticed? he asked.
How had you not noticed?

Red Circle

On the platform at West Hampstead
I saw an ad for an exhibition
which included your work.
I pictured myself at the gallery,
dark glasses, collar up, a mysterious
patron leaving red 'sold' circles
in her wake. When we met,
it was your light I was sold on,
as much as your green eyes,
your Levi's. I may as well have stuck
a red circle on my forehead –
from the first day no one else
got a look in. Van Gogh wrote
that his sunflowers were an expression
of gratitude for the Yellow House.
I see him in that Provençal light
which strips away the layer
that protects us from beauty.
Almond blossom, stars, cypresses.
Wheatfields, crows. What will I see
when one day I stand in front of you again?

Hero

I chose one of the Greek islands
to return to again and again,
somewhere sanctioned by Lawrence Durrell
who lived post-war in a house
next to the Islamic graveyard.
I give the Villa Cleobolus a nod
each time I pass, imagining Durrell
and Eve on the terrace where now
there are only cats spilling over
from the graveyard – the one-eyed,
the lame, the nursing queens,
each and every one fur and bones.
I thought I'd been clever,
thinking surely I wouldn't nurse
the lack of you somewhere
we'd never been together.
Yet as I swam back to shore today
I saw you. *What if?* I asked myself,
waves pushing me under on a day
I'd never needed a hero more.

The Joke

The cleaning staff are so kind to me,
they treat me like royalty or like their pet,
patting me on the head when I pass
the laundry room where they smoke and chat.
A woman travelling alone in a country
where so few travel alone – they fuss,
they advise. And then it occurs to me –
on top of the pile of books in my room
they've seen your photo and they think,
'Her son, how handsome, and she keeps
his photo with her, God willing he isn't dead,'
because my bedside table could be a shrine:
the photo, the Celtic cross, a handful of petals,
candles, and rose quartz for love in the heart.
You are frozen in the photo at twenty-four,
and I am sixty, so if I'd given birth to you
I'd have been the same age as my mother
when she gave birth to me. Oh, how I soared
in the cleaning staff's estimation! Not just
a woman of a certain age travelling alone,
but a mother, a woman with some status,
and a woman who might be grieving.
As they bleach my balcony floor and smooth
the bed linen, do I lack for anything, they ask?
And you smile and smile as though you are in on the joke.
And I pat you on the head each time I pass.

Films We Saw at *The Phoenix*

Diva, The Unbearable Lightness of Being,
Farewell My Concubine, Annie Hall, Manhattan.
My neighbour called it 'life's rich tapestry',
that real-life day you drove off in a packed van.
You left behind a wardrobe of naked hangers,
bare walls, half-empty shelves of books collapsing.
It doesn't work out for Annie and Alvy either,
but in the last scene they meet in a diner
to talk about and treasure it all – the lobsters,
the spider in the bath, *The Sorrow and the Pity*,
that very first game of doubles, walking
by the Hudson at dawn – weaving the threads together,
spreading it out tenderly, the tapestry
of their love which they alone could see.

Aftermath

We used to visit the house where I now live,
so there are photos of you playing on the patio
with my nephews. Fathers now themselves,
they have long forgotten you, forgotten the love
of being lifted on your shoulders, how they'd fight
until they cried for another turn. In other photos
you are helping to worm lambs, shear sheep,
or you are in the orchard, balancing in apple trees.
I wonder if you enjoyed any of it?
Because it was what the men in my family did
– mucking in – I'm sorry to say I never asked.
But I stood back to take those photos as though
some part of me didn't trust it could go on, the luck,
the windfall of good fortune in having found you,
that sooner or later I'd be shorn of it.
And a photograph of the patio today would be
a still life – a woman in a wide-brimmed hat,
pots of lavender, a table and chairs.
All commotion over. No fights, no begging
for attention, no strong desires
either way for anything; no more weeping
with frustration, anger or grief.
It's someone else's turn, that's all.

Beauty Spot

Let it be the other way round,
let your wife have met you first
in your early twenties, not a penny
to your name or hers. Let her ride out
that decade, the searching, the constant
restlessness, changing address almost
a religion. Formal education over
but what form will your lives take?
And let her be faced with the *to be*
or not to be of children, not meet you
when maturity has intervened.
And then let a parent die, die
young, let it remap the earth
so she has to learn how to walk again,
and let you decide to stay, not to run,
but it's hard to see her at her worst,
and remember neither of you
have a penny, it's month to month,
address to address, and throw several
countries into the mix, why not.
And you are both still thinking of each place,
each job this can't be it, what's the next
religion whilst losing sight of the religion
that you are to each other, how you met
in a white city on a gilt-edged day
when she thought 'Who's that?' and you thought
'Who's that?' and you went dancing
to Madonna singing 'Who's that?'
And later let no one – including you – tell her
that she's changed, that you're lonely
and that she'll lose you if she doesn't absorb
how self-absorbed she is,
that you'll look elsewhere and meet me
one regular day at work,

and I don't want to write, I'm not in therapy,
I'm not bereaved and all my life
I've watched my mother loving my father,
I know how it's done. It was raining, though,
and not even poetic rain, just nothingy
half-cock Oxford rain, and Madonna
had already been several Madonnas
since she sang 'Who's that girl?',
with her platinum hair, her dark brows,
her beauty spot.

Bringing Things Forward

I wish I'd concertinaed things,
brought them forward – not Alexandria
one day, but Alexandria this spring;
returning to Thrace one day – no,
returning in June; Tarifa, Tangier –
in the autumn cool. Monet's garden,
Frida's *Casa Azul*, long weeks
in Greece, swimming off rocks
into tilting cobalt blue, splashing out
on the kind of place where lemon trees
shade the terrace, where stone lions
sleep on duty, where lunch
begins at three and doesn't know
when to end. All this I day-dreamt
for us: Rembrandt's Amsterdam,
Vermeer's Delft, everyone's Rome.
And when at home in a 9-5 sort of way,
champagne on a random Monday
just because, no 'saving for later'.
My parents would bring champagne
home from France then never find
the effervescence to open it.
Even in her eighties, my mother
was saving things for later,
saving things for best.
Lest we not live, lest we die,
lest there be no later,
lest there be only today,
lest it be nonsense to talk of
'bringing things forward'
when what comes forward
is the end.

That *Selige Sehnsucht* Feeling

I'd name it *Selige Sehnsucht*, that feeling
my home gave me yesterday, words
you used once in a note –
I must have forgotten something,
I have that Selige Sehnsucht *feeling.*
It's an indefinable ache – not melancholy,
not sorrow, and more sinuous than sadness –
a feeling on a journey, picking up
strands of other like-hearted feelings on its way.
Is it possible to be sick for home while still there?
I think you were saying you missed me
before you'd even left. And yesterday,
as the red sun lowered, picking up other reds
on its way – flame red, orange red, ember red –
I ached for what I was looking at:
the long tawny-brown grass which,
from across the field, the house seemed
to grow out of putting me in mind
of an Edward Hopper house in a timeless
American field and the house retreating
into itself in the restful silence.
The bats came out. A barn owl flew close.
And the wind which often stirs at the end
of a summer's day stirred. Take the place from me,
I almost thought, so I can have the memory
and be through the loss itself.
Was it something similar, a feeling in the same family
of feelings, that prompted your use of *Selige Sehnsucht*
in that long-ago note? *I must have forgotten something,*
you wrote, though whatever it was that was
taking you away for a few nights hadn't even begun:
Or is it just that I love you so?

NOTES

'The Eve of St Agnes' (12)
Lines 22-26 are lifted from various stanzas in the original poem by Keats.

Mozart's 233rd Birthday (15)
Gettoni: Tokens for use in Italian public phones
'Con tutto il sapore dei giorni più belli': With all the flavour of the most beautiful days

Qui e Li (18)
Here and There

ACKNOWLEDGEMENTS

My gratitude to Justine Palmer and the Royal Literary Fund for timely and generous financial aid. My thanks to my editor, Neil Astley, and everyone at Bloodaxe. And a special thank you to Bernard O'Donoghue for his encouragement over many years.